Illustrations by Lorand Golebiowski
Graphic Project by VZNstudio

Dedicated to any and all readers who are interested in the possibility of a different way of living. May you find this book useful for your growth.

Thank you to my incredibly loving and supportive wife, who is always there for us all and who has helped in so many aspects of getting this book together. Thank you to my two wonderful sons who are full of life and who continually inspire me in every way. Thank you to Priya Ishaya for her advice and encouragement in the creation of this book. Thank you to my teacher Maharishi Krishnananda Ishaya who continues to guide me unwaveringly and whose love and dedication are without limits.

WHAT IS INNER PEACE?

Unmask the mystery of the present moment. See how it will change your life and begin your transformation now, with a daily self-help journal included.

Introduction

So many people have asked me about my experience of inner peace and then assumed they know exactly what I'm talking about when they hear my description of it. An extremely rare few who have their own practice have had some idea. But the truth is, the absolute vast majority have no idea at all what I am talking about – even though they think they do.

If they did, they would instantly drop everything and run to the nearest meditation class or seek a path to truth for all they were worth. Because the reality of a pure experience of inner peace is so far beyond any kind of mental description, so far beyond any idea that the intellect might have of beauty, of joy, of wonder, of love, that it cannot be understood with words. It can only be experienced. And that experience is completely unimaginable to one who has not yet had a taste of it. I mean ***completely***.

I had no idea what I was doing when I signed up for my first meditation course, which I did almost by accident. I quite liked the idea of meditation as long as it was something that fitted within my routine, but really the only thing I wanted at the time was to be a bit calmer and happier, maybe.

But what I have discovered over time, the experience I have now, is so much greater than anything I could have ever imagined even in my wildest of dreams. However, it can hardly be conveyed. If you are reading this, I am assuming that you don't have an experience of inner peace, otherwise you probably wouldn't have bought the book. But I want you to experience it with all my heart. And so I have done my best, using an analogy of climbing a mountain to help you see, give you some hint of what might be possible in the hope that you will be inspired to pursue this experience.

Each chapter describes new levels of clarity experienced when consciousness expands. As the experience of becoming more conscious is imperceivable to one who has not yet experienced it, each chapter is structured around the analogy of climbing up a mountain and, at each stage, perceiving what previously could not be perceived.

Throughout the book, and at the end of it, there are exercises that are inspired by over 20 years of practising and teaching meditation. If you do them with commitment and to the best of your ability, these will help you greatly to begin to step into an experience of inner peace. This may be fleeting initially, but the exercises are in any case directing you towards that experience; they are pointers to the truth. Then it is up to you to continue, as I will explain further on in the book.

I would advise you to read one chapter per day. If you read the chapter in the morning, you can then practise the exercise in that chapter during that same day; if you read the chapter in the evening, you can do the exercise the following day. Alternatively, you can read the whole book and then go back and do each exercise, one day at a time.

. 1

When we are on the ground, we are lost in the forest. There isn't much perspective.

The average human is not really here.

We worry about AI and about sharing our world with entities that have vast knowledge and capabilities but no conscience or consciousness. But the reality is, this is also a pretty close description of most humans today. We have access to vast amounts of information but are not very conscious of ourselves most of the time. The average conversation consists of regurgitated facts and opinions that we read or heard somewhere and that we believe to be true. Our opinions are the opinions of others, which are a mishmash of the opinions of others again. We are all really just repeating stuff in ever more fragmented combinations (while believing it to be ours). Even our commentary on our personal experience is mired in distortion from our individual programming. What we have experienced in life so far has an almost absolute effect on how we perceive things today. We are not seeing what's really there, unfiltered; we are looking, hearing, even tasting and smelling things through our conditioning and programming.

Today (or tomorrow, if you're reading this at night), have the intention to notice your tendencies to criticise, your judgements, whether good or bad, and your opinions. No need to do anything with them. Just notice them. Write them down on the page opposite.

I am judging & critiasing Ian because of how his behaviour has been.

I generally don't judge anyone, I just let them be.

. 2

We move a bit higher up the mountain, and we realise that the trees have tops to them and that above them is the sky.

When we begin on our spiritual path,
we start to notice things.

We start to see things that had previously been completely imperceivable to us. These may be small things, subtle things to begin with. We might notice that we have a tendency to behave in a certain way around certain types of people or a certain person. We may notice that there are specific moments when we feel insecure. We may notice that we have a tendency to worry about something that is completely beyond our control and that, usually, does not present a problem in the end anyway. We may start to be more attentive to others as we engage with them; we may also become aware that others are victims of the same or similar mental patterns as those we are starting to become aware of in ourselves. So, we start to wake up a bit and see a slightly more complete reality around us. And, of course, in seeing these things, we also start to question how it was possible that we couldn't see them before.

HOMEWORK #2

For the next day, have the intention to be aware of yourself. When you notice that you are getting caught up in thinking, worrying or feeling awkward around a certain person, just STOP. And become aware. Write down briefly what happened here.

I did find myself thinking about how I'd feel if I got an e-mail or a message from Ian today. It makes me feel so on edge, fearful, anxious, angry etc.

use this page for homework

**Higher up still,
we see that even
the trees are only
a carpet of green in
a much wider world.
We can perhaps
see a beautiful
ancient temple
in the distance.**

As we grow in consciousness,
we become aware of still more.

What previously seemed to be an absolute solid reality is now questionable at best. As we go about our day, we become aware of concepts and beliefs that we have held onto. These may be beliefs about ourselves, about others, about our country, our work, our profession, our culture, even our religion. We start to see the games people play – and the games that we have been playing, with ourselves and with others. We may realise that things we have always wanted are not really what we want at all, and that these previous desires were really just the product of what others expected of us, expected us to want or told us directly that we should want – a certain educational pathway, a certain type of job, a certain income or a certain way of life, for example. So, slowly, we start to become free of our programming, free to experience a new level of reality.

HOMEWORK #3

For the next day, have the intention to see where your beliefs and desires come from. Are those beliefs true? How do you know? And what about what you want? Are you sure you want it? Did the desire come from within you, or was it subtly fed to you by some external factor or person?

I feel that my beliefs are at my core. They relate to my values. Not born from external influences.

use this page for homework

And we keep going. Now we can see that there is a huge lake far away, and that the sun is shining down on all the world.

So, we have already seen much.

By now, most of the big things regarding our programming have been revealed. There is already a huge sense of freedom; we are no longer chained to petty desires and pre-programmed systems as we climb still higher. Now begin realisations regarding the more subtle aspects of our limitations and programmes. There is still more to be revealed. We continue to perceive subtle reactions in ourselves and small preferences that we hadn't noticed before. The world around us takes on a more enhanced reality as our senses are no longer constrained by labels, opinions or constant thinking. Eating may become an altogether more conscious experience as we are now able to taste the ingredients within each recipe. Sounds are enhanced, and we may even start to hear sounds or melodies within our daily life that had previously completely passed us by. We start to appreciate the beauty in all things. We feel gratitude for so much of what is in our lives. We feel love – no longer the kind of possessive, exchanging type of love that is so common in the world today, but a kind of unconditional love, a true desire to be there for people and to help people with no personal reward. We see the tenderness in all people, sometimes hiding far beneath the surface. We start to experience true selflessness and the incredible expansion that that brings.

HOMEWORK #4

For the next day, practise gratitude. Write down 10 things or people that you are grateful for in your life. Things or people whose simple existence you are grateful for. Things or people that you do not want or need anything from but that you are grateful for. This is a lovely exercise to repeat now and again, whenever you remember.

1. Moonns
2. Poops
3. Cj
4. Nj
5. Jfu
6. Sarah P
7. Kay
8. Becca
9. V f S
10. Skye & Star

& Many more!

♡

use this page for homework

·5

Still higher, we can see a much more complete reality: sea, land, sun and sky all working together in harmony.

As we grow further, we start to place less
emphasis on the things around us
even our own bodies.

These things are still very much part of our experience and there for us to appreciate and enjoy. But they start to lose their seriousness or realness. Our internal reality becomes far greater, far more delightful and far more real and true. But it is very important to note that this doesn't mean we withdraw from the external world – far from it. Our continuing expansion and experience of inner peace becomes a kind of platform from which to live. We start to see what life is like completely unaffected by our previous programming and by the collective programming of the world. We are now free to see and live in the present moment and, while our internal experience is golden, we also discover that this is by far the most efficient way to live in the external world. We are out of the way. We can help others, be of service and be aligned with truly useful purpose.

For the next day, practise placing less emphasis on your material world. Appreciate everything that you want to appreciate, enjoy it and be grateful for it, but notice when you are making your happiness dependent on it. If you are particularly grateful for or attached to something or someone, imagine what you would be like without that thing or person. Would you be any less you?

I am more appreciate of people in my life, animals, books etc.
I have noticed how much less reliant on buying 'things' I am now for happiness. I know why.

use this page for homework

.6

And still there is more. We can now see the curve of the earth and perhaps, as twilight approaches, that the sun is not the only star.

It does not even stop here.

As we grow still further and dedicate our life to waking up, we are showered with divine gifts, the likes of which are literally unimaginable from what may be called 'the sleep state' down on the forest floor. How can someone who lives in the undergrowth and has spent their entire life there begin to have any idea of what is above the treetops, let alone what is far away in the distance or up in the infinite sky? Just as our mountain climber starts to perceive things that were completely impossible to perceive from the forest floor, such as the curve of the earth and the vastness of space beyond our planet, the awake person continually becomes aware of things that were simply not possible to have any experience of while trapped in the sleep state.

Let go of your beliefs about life. For today, imagine that you are visiting this planet for the first time. Watch, observe, notice. Make no judgements – to the best of your ability :). Just observe with love and curiosity. Write down what you discover.

use this page for homework

• 7

Rising still higher, we can see that even the earth itself is small compared to the infinite beyond.

Our experience is now rooted in the present moment and all the joy that brings.

And just as the mountain climber, nearing the summit, must be increasingly careful of where they put their next foot, we must be increasingly vigilant to distraction and the wavering of our commitment to waking up. The mind becomes increasingly subtle and may find artful ways to trick us back into ignorance, so commitment to our priority is increasingly important if we want to continue growing.

How much more is there to see?

Becoming more present and waking up can be the sweetest thing. It can be simple, it can be enjoyable, it can be fun. And it can certainly be an incredible adventure. The only thing that is really required is for us to realise our highest priority and remain true to that without distraction, to the best of our ability. To accept the direction and flow of what comes next, rather than resisting it. And to always be open to feedback from our fellow explorers. It is important to remain humble and never think that we know, as we never will. We may have 'aha' moments, perceptions of a higher reality, but the important thing is to continue to let go of them all. As soon as we think we've got it, we are lost again.

Your final homework is to answer this question:
If you could have one wish, and only one – so, your highest desire – what would it be?

(Tip: think big :))

Write it down in big letters here.

use this page for homework

Afterword

Do not delude yourself that you can wake up to truth all by yourself if you talk about it a lot, read books on enlightenment and practise the odd technique now and again when you feel spiritually inspired. It doesn't work like that. Although there are many techniques and books that can be helpful and inspiring, they are only really pointing you in the right direction (this book included). If you want to get out of the undergrowth and climb up the mountain, you need a valid teaching and a guide.

It is very comfortable to think that you can do it on your own, reading books and picking up spiritual concepts, but this will only serve to help you become 'mentally' enlightened at best. If you are curious about the real thing, about moving beyond the concepts and experiencing it for yourself, you need to prioritise that and find a valid teaching and teacher. Just by making it your number one priority, you are already taking a huge leap towards your own growth. When the student is ready, the teacher (in whatever form it may take) appears.

But it needn't be hard. In fact, usually, the more we try, the more difficult it becomes. We simply need to make it a priority and we may then find that the universe unfolds to bring us what we want, in ways that we may never have suspected.

A word of warning, however – if you declare that you want to wake up, you will likely find that things start moving in that direction, but they may not move in the way that you imagined. Things may start happening very differently from how you would have planned them, and resistance to this will only slow your growth and become uncomfortable. But if you go with it, growth can be extremely quick.

If you want to wake up, allow life to show you the most direct route. Life knows what it's doing. Be open to what is presented and be willing to let go of everything that you are not. Decide first on your highest priority and then see what happens.

MOUNTAIN CLIMBERS ONLY BEYOND THIS POINT!

If you want to grow – and you may not; you may opt for the comfortable option and decide that you are fine as you are, in which case please stop reading here – but if you do want to climb the mountain, the following pages form a brief journal to help you take action and begin your journey. Use it to continue your exploration and record your discoveries over the next two weeks to keep you focused on your own growth while you look for a suitable teaching.

We will base each daily theme on one or part of the seven exercises outlined in the first part of this book, but we will go into aspects of them in more depth, sometimes covering a single theme and sometimes a particular aspect of a theme.

Tendencies. Which personal tendencies are you aware of? Write them all down as far as you can remember, even the little ones. Do you procrastinate? Do you continually put things off until another time, such as a diet, fitness schedule or awkward situation that you need to confront? Are you often anxious about interactions with certain people? Are you fearful of certain things that haven't happened yet and that may never happen?

Again, just write them down here and let go of any judgements around these tendencies to the best of your ability. You probably share them with most of humanity anyway. And please don't judge yourself if you feel that you can't let go of your judgements around them! It doesn't matter; we are just writing them down to become more aware of them.

use this page for homework

Judgements. Whether you realise it or not, we are constantly judging everything about our life experience. Was your coffee (or tea) bitter this morning, or was it delicious? Better than yesterday? Did you decide someone was arrogant, or someone else insincere? Are some people idiots? Are others quite simply wrong? What is wrong with the *world*? Can you see your judgements around that?

Write down as many as possible here. Again, it doesn't matter! You are not a bad person for judging! It is simply a tendency of humanity; it is almost hard-wired into society. And so, we write them down to become aware of this aspect of ourselves. It can be a journey of discovery. Don't judge your judgements :)!

use this page for homework

Become aware. For today, practise just stopping. When you remember, pull out from the constant thoughts and mental or emotional activity and focus on this moment. Notice that this moment is here, and that it is happening. Allow this moment to be exactly as it is. Don't try to change it. What did you notice? Was there peace in this moment? Is there peace now in this moment? Write down whatever comes to you to describe this moment now.

use this page for homework

Desires. Write down five big desires that you have in your life. Label them one to five; they don't have to be in any order. Now, take each one and write down why you desire it. If you had it, or if it happened, what would that bring to your life, or to others' lives?

Did any of your five desires come from the same overall desire – for example, the desire to simply be happy or at peace?

use this page for homework

Gratitude. Today we will repeat the exercise from the fourth homework. Write down 10 things that you are grateful for today. It's nice to do this before you go to bed at night, but you can do it at any time in the day.

use this page for homework

The material and physical world. Look at the things in your physical world that you are most proud of, that you most appreciate, especially those things that you would find it difficult to be without. These could be objects and possessions, but they may also be to do with your body or personality. Do you especially love your hairstyle? Are you proud of your looks? Perhaps you are an athlete and proud of your body? Do you have an outgoing character that you value highly? They may also be other people. Are there people in your life whom you think you could not live without? Write down everything that comes to mind here. Now, imagine how it would be if those things, personal qualities or people disappeared. Would you still be *you* inside? After all, when did you become *you* inside? Or have you always been *you*?

use this page for homework

HOMEWORK #14

Observe. Today, just observe life happening around you. It's okay to get caught up in your own actions if you are focusing on something – perhaps your work or a job that you have to do, such as looking after children or relatives, for example – but when you remember, just observe with pure curiosity, as if you were an alien visiting the planet for the first time. Just for today, pretend you know nothing about anything, as though your mind is a blank slate. Write down what you observe here.

use this page for homework

Remind yourself of your highest desire. If it has changed, no problem – just write it down here. Write it down also if it hasn't changed.

use this page for homework

Now we will shift up a gear and bring some interaction with these themes into our day.

So today, practise being kind. You could try this all day with whoever you meet, or it could just be one person in one moment. Whatever you feel comfortable with. In that moment when you are playing with being kind, let go of any personal judgements about whether the person deserves it or not. And just be kind. You might simply smile at a person who is angry. You might offer encouragement. You might listen. You might help someone. It really doesn't matter what happens; only the intention is important.

use this page for homework

Praise someone. This doesn't have to be worship! Just appreciate. If a taxi driver gets you somewhere efficiently, let them know that you appreciate their effort. If someone at the checkout is pleasant, tell them how great it is to be served by someone who is kind. Find things to appreciate wherever you go. Be alert to the possibilities of appreciation. Again, you could praise just one person or many. It doesn't matter.

use this page for homework

HOMEWORK #18

Thank someone. Not as a matter of course, but sincerely, if you are truly grateful for it. And also try to be alert to what you are grateful for. If you are aware, you might realise that you are grateful for the person who serves your morning coffee, but perhaps you have never said so other than uttering a standard "thanks" when they hand it to you. So, play with being just a bit more profound in your gratitude. For example, you might say something like, "Thanks so much. Your morning coffee is always the best; it changes my day!"

use this page for homework

FOR PRO CLIMBERS ONLY

Next, we are taking this one small step further. You are now going to practise acceptance of all parts of your life experience. It is one thing to be appreciative of and kind to those people and things that you like. But the next step is being appreciative of those people and things that you are not so keen on.

HOMEWORK #19

For today, be kind to someone you don't like. If you really want to play with this, you can be kind to more than one person whom you don't like! But one is plenty :)
What did you notice?

use this page for homework

HOMEWORK #20

Praise someone you want to complain about. A small tip: Leave aside the list of things that you want to complain about regarding this person and find something about them that you can appreciate. Just consciously notice that you have an option to appreciate or to complain. And choose to appreciate this time. What did you notice?

use this page for homework

Thank someone for their efforts whom you don't feel deserves it. Everyone is really only doing their best. No one is you, so you can't know what that other person's experience of life is like. Therefore, you cannot judge them. There may be many things that you think they are doing wrong, but try to see some small thing that you could be grateful for. It might be something as simple as their presence, which might just remind you of how lucky you are to not be in their shoes. What did you notice?

use this page for homework

If you are open to a suggestion, then I can of course not recommend highly enough the teachings of The Bright Path Ishayas (www.thebrightpath.com), whose guidance has been, and continues to be, everything in my journey.

I do not know of any other teaching that is as effective as this one in terms of guiding one to let go of all that is not true. But this is only a suggestion.

The path is yours.

About the Author

Marc Krusin is a dedicated father, husband, designer and Ishaya monk. He has been meditating for over 20 years and teaching the Bright Path Ishaya's Ascension since 2011, during which time he has helped hundreds of people live happier, more fulfilling, and more present lives. Marc is always inspired by people who are committed to waking up. In addition to teaching Ascension and designing, he loves mountains and skiing, sea and sailing, food, and great company.

About the Illustrator

Lorand Golebiowski is a designer and animator based in Sydney, Australia. He met Marc while living in London and collaborated with him on a range of projects for The Bright Path and other clients. He continues to work internationally in design and animation from his studio in Sydney. When not creating, he enjoys skateboarding and video games.

Printed in Great Britain
by Amazon

57616787R00056